MEDITERRANEAN DIET COOKBOOK FOR SENIORS 2024

The Complete Simple and Easy Delicious Recipes with Nutritional Information and a 30-Day Meal Plan.

Dr.Stephen Campbell

Book belongs to

TABLE OF CONTENTS

All Recipes with
ingredient
instruction
prep time
serving size &
nutritional information

INTRODUCTION

Dr. Stephen Campbell's Journey: A Testament to Mediterranean Brilliance

Dr. Stephen Campbell, a seasoned nutritionist with decades of experience, found himself standing at a crossroads when it came to his own well-being. Despite his extensive knowledge of nutrition, the demands of a busy life had taken a toll on his health, leaving him searching for a path back to vitality. It was then that the "Mediterranean Diet Cookbook for Seniors 2024" found its way into his hands, becoming not just a guide but a transformative companion on his journey to renewed health.

The Wake-Up Call

In the midst of his hectic schedule, Dr. Campbell realized that his own health had taken a back seat. Long hours, irregular meals, and the challenges of modern life had resulted in fatigue and a sense of depletion. It was time for a change, and that change began with the wisdom of the Mediterranean diet.

The Transformative Power of the Cookbook

Chapter 1: The Mediterranean Magic Unveiled

Dr. Campbell was captivated by the insights into the Mediterranean lifestyle. As he absorbed the foundational principles, he realized that this wasn't just a diet—it was a holistic approach to living.

Chapter 2: A Culinary Sojourn Through Mediterranean History
The historical context provided a profound appreciation for the cultural richness woven into each dish. Dr. Campbell found himself transported through time, connecting with the traditions that had sustained generations.

Chapter 3: Mindful Nutrition for Seniors
Tailored nutritional insights addressed Dr. Campbell's specific needs. The inclusion of cognitive health strategies struck a chord, aligning seamlessly with his desire for holistic well-being.

Chapter 4: Decoding the 30-Day Meal Plan
The meticulously crafted meal plan became Dr. Campbell's culinary compass. It not only offered variety and flavor but also became a tool for mindful eating and balanced nutrition.

A Culinary Renaissance

Dr. Campbell embraced the cookbook's recipes with gusto, infusing his kitchen with the vibrant aromas of the Mediterranean. From hearty breakfasts to flavorful dinners, each dish became a celebration of good health. His energy levels soared, and the Mediterranean diet's emphasis on whole foods and lean proteins brought about a noticeable change in his overall vitality.

A True-Life Story: Finding Inspiration in Wellness

Amidst Dr. Campbell's personal transformation, a heartwarming true-life story in the cookbook struck a chord. The narrative of a senior whose life had taken a positive turn through the Mediterranean diet resonated deeply. It wasn't just a story; it was a testament to the profound impact that intentional dietary choices could have on one's well-being.

Beyond the Pages: Dr. Campbell's Ongoing Journey

As the pages of the cookbook turned, Dr. Campbell found himself not just following a diet but adopting a lifestyle. The Mediterranean way of living, with its emphasis on fresh, seasonal produce, mindful eating, and the joy of shared meals, became a guiding principle in his daily life.

The Ripple Effect

Dr. Campbell's journey didn't go unnoticed. His colleagues and patients observed the transformative impact of the Mediterranean diet on his well-being. He became a living testament to the principles outlined in the cookbook, inspiring those around him to explore the richness of this lifestyle.

A Grateful Reflection

As Dr. Campbell reflects on his journey, he acknowledges the pivotal role that the "Mediterranean Diet Cookbook for Seniors 2024" played in his renaissance. It wasn't just a collection of recipes; it was a guide that rekindled his passion for wholesome living.

The story of Dr. Stephen Campbell serves as a beacon of inspiration for anyone seeking a path to vitality and well-being. His journey, intertwined with the wisdom of the Mediterranean diet, is a reminder that it's never too late to embrace a lifestyle that nourishes both the body and the soul.

✸ A Big Thank You for Joining This Tasty Journey! ❦

Hello there,

I really want to thank you for choosing to explore the delicious adventure in the "Mediterranean Diet Cookbook for Seniors." It's not just about getting recipes; it shows your commitment to a healthier and happier life.

Your presence makes this journey rich and exciting. As someone who loves putting passion into each page, I'm so happy you've decided to be part of this adventure.

Now, as we go through these tasty recipes, I invite you to take a moment—share your thoughts and experiences. Your feedback is like a treasure map guiding me to make things even better for those who come after you.

Your voice is important and shapes the story of this cooking adventure. Every word you share can inspire and connect with others who haven't discovered the magic in these pages yet. It's not just a review; it's a gift to others looking for a way to be healthy and happy.

So, could you take a moment to write down your thoughts? Tell me about the flavors you liked, the recipes that became your favorites, and the moments that made you smile. Your words aren't just for me; they help build a community of food lovers, each adding their unique touch to a happy and healthy life.

As you enjoy the good feelings after a tasty meal from this cookbook, know that your words can reach beyond your kitchen. They can inspire others to enjoy every meal and make every day a chance for well-being.

Thank you for more than just picking a cookbook. Thank you for becoming a part of a group of people who love good food and want to live a vibrant life.

With gratitude,

★★★★★

[Dr. Campbell's]
Publisher of the "Mediterranean Diet Cookbook for Seniors"

Chapter 2: Understanding the Mediterranean Diet

To truly embrace the Mediterranean diet, one must understand its roots deeply embedded in the fertile soil of history and tradition. Originating from the countries that surround the Mediterranean Sea, this diet is more than a set of guidelines; it's a way of life that has sustained generations. As we embark on this culinary expedition, let's explore the tradition that forms the foundation of the Mediterranean diet.

The History and Origin of the Mediterranean Diet: A Culinary Odyssey

The Mediterranean diet is not just a collection of recipes; it's a living testament to the history, culture, and resilience of the people who have thrived around the Mediterranean Sea for centuries. To understand the roots of this celebrated diet, we must embark on a culinary odyssey that spans time and geography, uncovering the rich tapestry of traditions that have shaped the way we eat today.

Ancient Beginnings

The origins of the Mediterranean diet can be traced back to the cradle of civilization itself. In the ancient civilizations of Egypt, Greece, and Rome, the abundance of the Mediterranean's fertile lands and bountiful seas laid the foundation for a diet that would stand the test of time. The ancient Greeks, particularly, held a profound appreciation for the relationship between food, health, and well-being.

Grains and Olive Oil: Staples of Antiquity

In ancient Greece, grains such as barley and wheat formed the basis of the daily diet. These grains were not only sustenance but also held cultural and religious significance. Paired with the golden elixir of the Mediterranean — olive oil — these staples became the cornerstone of nutrition.

Olive oil, with its versatile uses in cooking and dressing, represented more than just a source of healthy fats. It became a symbol of wealth, fertility, and peace. The olive tree, often referred to as the "tree of life," held a revered place in Greek mythology, further emphasizing the profound connection between food and culture.

Influence of Ancient Rome

As the Roman Empire expanded its dominion over the Mediterranean region, culinary traditions evolved, incorporating a diverse array of ingredients from conquered lands. The Roman diet became a mosaic of flavors, blending the simplicity of Mediterranean staples with exotic spices, fruits, and grains from distant territories.

The Culinary Crossroads

The port city of Rome served as a culinary crossroads where ingredients from Africa, Asia, and Europe converged. This cultural exchange not only enriched the Roman diet but also laid the groundwork for the diverse and inclusive nature of the Mediterranean diet we know today.

Middle Ages: Preserving Tradition Amidst Turmoil

The fall of the Roman Empire marked the beginning of the Middle Ages, a period characterized by social upheaval and economic decline. Yet, amidst the turmoil, the culinary traditions of the Mediterranean endured, anchored by the resilience of communities dependent on the land and sea for sustenance.

Monastic Gardens and Culinary Alchemy

During this era, monastic gardens became havens for the cultivation of herbs, fruits, and vegetables. Monks, often the keepers of knowledge during a time of widespread illiteracy, experimented with culinary alchemy, refining the art of preserving and enhancing flavors. The monastic influence on Mediterranean cuisine laid the groundwork for the emphasis on fresh, locally sourced ingredients that defines the diet today.

Renaissance and the Age of Exploration

The Renaissance witnessed a revival of interest in the classical arts and sciences, sparking a renewed appreciation for the wisdom of ancient cultures. Simultaneously, the Age of Exploration opened new horizons, bringing exotic foods such as tomatoes, peppers, and potatoes to the shores of the Mediterranean.

Tomatoes and the Italian Renaissance

The arrival of tomatoes in Europe, often associated with Italian cuisine, marked a transformative moment in Mediterranean cooking. Initially met with skepticism due to its resemblance to poisonous nightshade, the tomato eventually became a central ingredient in dishes like pasta sauces and salads, contributing to the vibrant palette of Mediterranean flavors.

20th Century Revival: Ancel Keys and the Seven Countries Study

While the Mediterranean diet has ancient roots, its modern revival can be attributed in part to the pioneering work of Dr. Ancel Keys. In the aftermath of World War II, Dr. Keys initiated the landmark Seven Countries Study, which investigated the dietary habits and health outcomes of various populations.

The Key Findings

The study revealed a striking correlation between the traditional Mediterranean diet and lower rates of heart disease. The diet's emphasis on olive oil, fruits, vegetables, and lean proteins emerged as a beacon of health in stark contrast to the dietary patterns prevalent in other regions. Dr. Keys's advocacy for the Mediterranean diet laid the foundation for its recognition as a model for heart-healthy eating.

The Contemporary Mediterranean Diet

As we step into the 21st century, the Mediterranean diet has transcended its geographical boundaries to become a global phenomenon. Recognized by UNESCO as an Intangible Cultural Heritage, its principles extend far beyond the shores of the Mediterranean, resonating with individuals seeking not only a delicious way of eating but also a pathway to overall well-being.

Key Components of the Modern Mediterranean Diet

- Abundance of Plant-Based Foods:** Fruits, vegetables, legumes, nuts, and whole grains form the basis of meals, providing a wealth of vitamins, minerals, and antioxidants.

- Healthy Fats from Olive Oil:** Extra virgin olive oil, rich in monounsaturated fats, serves as the primary source of dietary fat, supporting heart health and reducing inflammation.

- Moderate Consumption of Dairy and Poultry:** Dairy products and poultry are enjoyed in moderation, contributing essential nutrients without overshadowing plant-based elements.

- Lean Proteins from Fish and Legumes:** Fish, a primary protein source, offers omega-3 fatty acids crucial for brain and heart health. Legumes provide an alternative plant-based protein.

- Emphasis on Fresh Herbs and Spices:** Herbs and spices not only enhance flavor but also offer additional health benefits, acting as natural seasonings with minimal reliance on salt.

- Moderate Wine Consumption: Red wine, consumed in moderation during meals, contributes antioxidants and complements the convivial atmosphere of shared dining.

A Timeless Legacy

The Mediterranean diet is not merely a historical relic; it's a living legacy that continues to evolve. Its resilience through the ages speaks to the profound connection between culture, environment, and well-being.

As we embrace the flavors and traditions of the Mediterranean, we participate in a culinary journey that transcends time, weaving the past into the present and sowing the seeds for a healthier future.

Core Principles

The Mediterranean diet is characterized by a set of fundamental principles that guide its composition. These principles not only contribute to the unique flavors but also underpin the health benefits associated with this lifestyle.

Abundance of Plant-Based Foods:

- Fruits, vegetables, legumes, nuts, and whole grains form the backbone of the diet, providing a rich array of vitamins, minerals, and antioxidants.

Healthy Fats from Olive Oil:

- Olive oil, a staple in Mediterranean kitchens, replaces saturated fats with monounsaturated fats, promoting heart health and reducing inflammation.

Moderate Consumption of Dairy and Poultry:

- Dairy and poultry are enjoyed in moderation, contributing essential nutrients without overshadowing the prominence of plant-based foods.

Lean Proteins from Fish and Legumes:

- Fish, a primary protein source, is rich in omega-3 fatty acids, supporting brain and heart health. Legumes provide an alternative protein source.

Emphasis on Fresh Herbs and Spices:
Herbs and spices not only add depth to dishes but also offer additional health benefits, acting as natural flavor enhancers.

Practical Tips for Seniors
For seniors embracing the Mediterranean diet, incorporating these principles into daily life can be both enjoyable and rewarding. Here are practical tips tailored to the unique needs of seniors:

Meal Planning for Nutrient-Rich Variety:
- Plan meals to include a variety of colorful fruits and vegetables to ensure a diverse range of nutrients.

Mindful Olive Oil Usage:
- Use extra virgin olive oil for cooking and dressing salads. Its monounsaturated fats can support joint health and reduce inflammation.

Adapting Protein Intake:
- Incorporate fish, legumes, and lean poultry into meals. These protein sources are easier on digestion while providing essential amino acids.

Herbs and Spices for Flavor and Health:
- Experiment with fresh herbs and spices to add flavor without excess salt, catering to seniors who may need to manage sodium intake.

Hydration Through Infusions:
- Stay hydrated with infused water using fresh herbs or slices of citrus. This ensures proper hydration, especially crucial for seniors.

Embracing the Mediterranean Lifestyle

Beyond the dietary aspects, the Mediterranean lifestyle encompasses various practices that contribute to overall well-being.

Physical Activity:

- Engage in moderate physical activity such as walking or gardening. This aligns with the active lifestyles of Mediterranean communities.

Mindful Eating:

- Practice mindful eating, savoring each bite and appreciating the flavors. This not only aids digestion but also enhances the enjoyment of meals.

Social Connection:

- Foster social connections through shared meals. Whether with family, friends, or neighbors, the act of communal dining adds a layer of joy to the Mediterranean diet.

Adapting the Mediterranean Diet to Your Lifestyle

As we delve into the subsequent chapters, keep in mind that the Mediterranean diet is not a rigid set of rules but a flexible and adaptable lifestyle. It's about embracing the abundance of nature, relishing the joy of shared meals, and savoring the flavors that have withstood the test of time.

Chapter 3: Health Benefits for Seniors: Nourishing the Mind and Body

In the previous chapters, we embarked on a journey through the history and roots of the Mediterranean diet, exploring its ancient origins and the cultural tapestry that shapes its essence. Now, as we transition to the heart of the matter, we delve into the health benefits that make the Mediterranean diet not only a culinary delight but also a prescription for vitality, particularly tailored to the well-being of seniors.

The Aging Paradigm: A Holistic Approach to Health
As individuals gracefully navigate the golden years, health becomes an ever-present consideration. The Mediterranean diet, with its emphasis on nutrient-dense, whole foods, emerges as a beacon of holistic well-being. Let's unravel the myriad health benefits that seniors can derive from adopting this time-tested lifestyle.

Cognitive Health: Nourishing the Brain

One of the standout features of the Mediterranean diet is its association with cognitive well-being. Numerous studies have explored the link between diet and cognitive decline, with compelling evidence suggesting that the Mediterranean diet may act as a shield against age-related cognitive impairment.

1. **Omega-3 Fatty Acids and Brain Health:**
   - Fish, a staple in the Mediterranean diet, is rich in omega-3 fatty acids. These essential fats are linked to improved cognitive function and a reduced risk of neurodegenerative diseases.

2. Antioxidants for Cognitive Resilience:

- The diet's abundance of fruits and vegetables provides a diverse range of antioxidants, which may help combat oxidative stress in the brain, a key factor in cognitive decline.

3. Moderate Wine Consumption and Cognitive Benefits:

- Resveratrol, a compound found in red wine, has been associated with enhanced cognitive function, further emphasizing the moderate consumption of wine in the Mediterranean lifestyle.

Heart Health: Nurturing the Cardiovascular System

Cardiovascular health is a paramount concern for seniors, and the Mediterranean diet offers a powerful ally in maintaining a healthy heart.

1.Monounsaturated Fats and Cardiovascular Support:

- Olive oil, a cornerstone of the diet, is abundant in monounsaturated fats. These heart-healthy fats contribute to lower cholesterol levels and reduced risk of heart disease.

2. Fiber-Rich Foods for Heart Health:

- Whole grains, fruits, and vegetables, prevalent in the Mediterranean diet, are rich in soluble fiber, which aids in managing cholesterol levels and promoting cardiovascular health.

3. Lean Proteins and Blood Pressure Control:

- The diet's emphasis on lean proteins, particularly from fish and legumes, contributes to maintaining healthy blood pressure levels, a critical aspect of heart health.

Managing Chronic Conditions: A Wholesome Approach
Seniors often grapple with chronic conditions, and the Mediterranean diet, with its anti-inflammatory and nutrient-dense nature, presents a promising approach to managing these health challenges.

1. Anti-Inflammatory Benefits:

- The diet's emphasis on fresh fruits, vegetables, and olive oil may contribute to reducing inflammation in the body, which is linked to various chronic conditions.

2. Weight Management and Diabetes:

- The Mediterranean diet's focus on whole, nutrient-dense foods supports healthy weight management, a crucial factor in managing diabetes and preventing complications.

3. Bone Health:

- Calcium-rich foods like dairy and leafy greens, combined with the diet's overall nutrient density, contribute to maintaining strong and healthy bones.

Practical Tips for Seniors: Tailoring the Mediterranean Lifestyle

Adopting the Mediterranean diet can be a transformative journey, and seniors can make this lifestyle shift with ease by incorporating practical tips into their daily routines.

1. Mindful Meal Planning:

- Plan meals that include a variety of colorful fruits and vegetables to ensure a diverse range of nutrients.
- Utilize herbs and spices for flavor without excess salt, catering to seniors who may need to manage sodium intake.

2. **Healthy Fats for Joint Health:**
   - Incorporate extra virgin olive oil into cooking and salad dressings for monounsaturated fats that support joint health and reduce inflammation.

3. **Protein for Digestive Ease:**
   - Include fish, legumes, and lean poultry for protein sources that are easier on digestion while providing essential amino acids.

4. **Hydration Through Infusions:**
   - Stay hydrated with infused water using fresh herbs or slices of citrus to ensure proper hydration, especially crucial for seniors.

5. **Mindful Eating Practices:**
   - Practice mindful eating, savoring each bite and appreciating the flavors, which aids digestion and enhances the enjoyment of meals.

Embracing the Lifestyle: A Blueprint for Senior Well-Being

As we navigate the unique health considerations of seniors, the Mediterranean diet emerges as more than just a set of guidelines—it becomes a blueprint for comprehensive well-being. From cognitive health to heart health and the management of chronic conditions, the diet offers a multifaceted approach to aging gracefully and healthfully.

Chapter 4: Setting Up Your Kitchen for Mediterranean Mastery

As we continue our exploration of the Mediterranean diet, we now turn our attention to the heart of the home—the kitchen. A well-equipped and thoughtfully arranged kitchen becomes the canvas for culinary creativity and the foundation for embracing the Mediterranean lifestyle. In this chapter, we'll guide you through the process of setting up your kitchen to embark on a journey filled with flavors, aromas, and the wholesome goodness of the Mediterranean diet.

The Mediterranean Kitchen: A Symphony of Ingredients
Before delving into the logistics of setting up your kitchen, let's take a moment to appreciate the core ingredients that form the soul of Mediterranean cuisine. These ingredients are not merely items on a shopping list; they are the building blocks of a culinary symphony that celebrates the richness of the land and the bounty of the sea.

1. Extra Virgin Olive Oil:

- Role: The backbone of Mediterranean cooking, used for sautéing, roasting, dressing salads, and adding a distinctive flavor to dishes.
- Selection Tip: Opt for cold-pressed, extra virgin olive oil for its robust flavor and high levels of antioxidants.

2. Fresh Herbs and Spices:

- Role: Elevate flavors and add depth to dishes without excessive use of salt.
- Essentials: Basil, oregano, thyme, rosemary, garlic, and parsley.
- Culinary Hack: Grow a small herb garden for a continuous supply of fresh herbs.

3. Whole Grains:

- Role: Provide a nutritious base for many Mediterranean dishes.
- Essentials: Farro, quinoa, bulgur, whole wheat couscous, and brown rice.
- Storage Tip: Keep grains in airtight containers to maintain freshness.

4. Fruits and Vegetables:

- Role: Essential for their vitamins, minerals, and antioxidants.
- Seasonal Choices: Tomatoes, bell peppers, eggplant, zucchini, lemons, oranges, and olives.
- Buying Guide: Opt for locally sourced and seasonal produce for maximum freshness.

5. Lean Proteins:

- Role: Serve as a primary source of protein while keeping the diet low in saturated fats.
- Choices: Fish (salmon, sardines, and tuna), legumes (lentils, chickpeas, and black beans), and lean poultry (chicken and turkey).
- Sustainable Sourcing: Choose sustainably caught fish and organic, pasture-raised poultry.

6. Dairy and Cheese:

- Role: Used sparingly, adding richness to certain dishes.
- Choices: Greek yogurt, feta cheese, and Parmesan.
- Quality Matters: Opt for high-quality, full-fat dairy products for a more indulgent flavor.

7. Nuts and Seeds:

- Role: Provide a crunchy texture and healthy fats.
- Options: Almonds, walnuts, pine nuts, and chia seeds.
- Storage Tip: Keep nuts and seeds in the refrigerator to prevent them from turning rancid.

Health Note: Consult with healthcare providers, especially for individuals with certain health conditions or medications.

Crafting Your Mediterranean Kitchen: Practical Tips

Now that we've acquainted ourselves with the essential ingredients, let's embark on creating your Mediterranean kitchen. The goal is to foster an environment that encourages creativity, accessibility, and a seamless integration of the Mediterranean lifestyle into your daily routine.

1. Organize Your Pantry:

- Categorize Essentials: Arrange your pantry with designated sections for grains, legumes, canned goods, and spices.
- Labeling: Use clear labels for easy identification of ingredients.

2. Invest in Quality Cookware:

- Essentials: A high-quality olive oil dispenser, non-stick pans, a sturdy chef's knife, and a set of stainless steel pots.
- Long-Term Investment: Quality cookware can enhance your cooking experience and last for years.

3. Create a Herb Garden:

- Location: Choose a sunny spot in your kitchen or balcony for herbs like basil, rosemary, and thyme.
- Potted Plants: Plant herbs in small pots for easy management and continuous supply.

4. Stock Up on Mason Jars:

- Storage Solution: Mason jars are ideal for storing grains, legumes, dried herbs, and homemade dressings.
- Aesthetic Appeal: The clear glass adds a touch of visual appeal to your pantry.

5. Incorporate Mediterranean Colors:

- Color Palette: Integrate earthy tones, such as olive green, rustic reds, and deep blues, into your kitchen decor.
- Visual Stimulation: These colors evoke the vibrant hues of Mediterranean landscapes.

6. Explore Mediterranean Cookbooks:

- Inspiration: Invest in a cookbook that delves into the intricacies of Mediterranean cuisine.
- Experimentation: Try new recipes regularly to expand your culinary repertoire.

7. Set Up a Mediterranean Meal Calendar:

- Weekly Planning: Designate specific days for Mediterranean-themed meals.
- Variety: Ensure diversity by exploring recipes from different Mediterranean regions.

Beyond the Kitchen: Embracing the Mediterranean Lifestyle

The Mediterranean lifestyle extends beyond the boundaries of your kitchen. It's a holistic approach that encompasses not only what you eat but also how you live. Here are some lifestyle tips to complement your culinary endeavors:

1. Active Living:

- Regular Exercise: Incorporate physical activity into your routine, such as walking, swimming, or gardening.
- Outdoor Connection: Spend time outdoors to align with the Mediterranean appreciation for nature.

2. Mindful Eating Practices:

- Savor Each Bite: Cultivate mindfulness during meals, enjoying the textures and flavors of each dish.
- Shared Meals: Whenever possible, dine with family or friends to foster a sense of community.

3. Hydration Rituals:

- Infused Water: Experiment with infused water using herbs, citrus slices, or cucumber.
- Herbal Teas: Enjoy herbal teas, such as chamomile or mint, as a soothing and hydrating beverage.

4. Social Connections:

- Community Events: Participate in community events or gatherings to foster social connections.
- Shared Activities: Engage in activities that bring people together, such as cooking classes or potluck dinners.

5. Restorative Practices:

- Quality Sleep: Prioritize a good night's sleep to support overall well-being.
- Relaxation Techniques: Explore relaxation practices, such as meditation or gentle yoga.

Your Mediterranean Haven: A Culinary Sanctuary
As you implement these practical tips and infuse your kitchen with the spirit of the Mediterranean, envision it not just as a cooking space but as a sanctuary of flavors and well-being. The Mediterranean lifestyle, with its emphasis on fresh, whole foods and a celebration of life's simple pleasures, becomes a daily ritual that nurtures both body and soul.

Chapter 5: Breakfast Delights Recipes

Breakfast Delights

Mediterranean Avocado Toast

Serving Size:2 10 minutes

INTRODUCTION

Start your day with a burst of Mediterranean flavors with this nutritious avocado toast. Creamy avocado, juicy tomatoes, and tangy feta cheese come together on a bed of whole-grain toast.

INGREDIENTS

- 1 ripe avocado
- 2 slices whole-grain bread
- 1 medium tomato, sliced
- 2 tbsp crumbled feta cheese
- Fresh basil leaves for garnish
- Salt and pepper to taste

INSTRUCTIONS

1. Toast the whole-grain bread slices to your liking.
2. Mash the ripe avocado and spread it evenly on the toasted bread.
3. Arrange tomato slices on top of the avocado.
4. Sprinkle crumbled feta cheese over the tomatoes.
5. Season with salt and pepper to taste.
6. Garnish with fresh basil leaves.
7. Serve immediately

NUTRITIONAL INFORMATION:

- Calories: 250 per serving
- Protein: 7g
- Fat: 15g
- Carbohydrates: 25g

Greek Yogurt Parfait with Berries

Serving Size:1 5 minutes

INTRODUCTION

Indulge in a wholesome Greek yogurt parfait filled with the sweetness of berries and the crunch of granola. This parfait is a delicious fusion of flavors and textures.

INGREDIENTS

- 1cup Greek yogurt
- 1/2 cup mixed berries (strawberries, blueberries, raspberries)
- 1/4 cup granola
- Drizzle of honey (optional)
- Fresh mint leaves for garnish

INSTRUCTIONS

1. In a glass or bowl, layer Greek yogurt.
2. Add a layer of mixed berries on top.
3. Sprinkle granola over the berries.
4. Repeat the layers.
5. Drizzle honey on the top layer if desired.
6. Garnish with fresh mint leaves.
7. Enjoy immediately.

NUTRITIONAL INFORMATION:

- Calories: 350 per serving
- Protein: 20g
- Fat: 10g
- Carbohydrates: 45g

Mediterranean Omelette

Serving Size:1 15 minutes

INTRODUCTION

Kickstart your morning with a protein-packed Mediterranean omelette. Filled with spinach, tomatoes, olives, and feta cheese, this omelette is a savory delight.

INGREDIENTS

- 3 eggs
- Handful of fresh spinach
- 1/2 cup cherry tomatoes, halved
- 2 tbsp Kalamata olives, sliced
- 2 tbsp crumbled feta cheese
- Salt and pepper to taste
- Olive oil for cooking

INSTRUCTIONS

1. Whisk the eggs in a bowl and season with salt and pepper.
2. Heat olive oil in a pan over medium heat.
3. Add fresh spinach and cherry tomatoes to the pan and sauté until wilted.
4. Pour the whisked eggs over the vegetables.
5. Sprinkle Kalamata olives and crumbled feta cheese evenly.
6. Cook until the edges set, then fold the omelette in half.
7. Slide onto a plate and serve.

NUTRITIONAL INFORMATION:

- Calories: 350 per serving
- Protein: 20g
- Fat: 25g
- Carbohydrates: 10g

Mediterranean Chia Seed Pudding

Serving Size:1

5 minutes (plus chilling time)

INTRODUCTION

Fuel your day with a nutrient-packed chia seed pudding infused with Mediterranean flavors. This make-ahead breakfast is not only delicious but also a great source of omega-3 fatty acids.

INGREDIENTS

- 3 tbsp chia seeds
- 1cup unsweetened almond milk
- 1/2 tsp vanilla extract
- 1 tbsp honey
- 1/4 cup mixed berries
- Sliced almonds for topping

INSTRUCTIONS

1. In a jar, mix chia seeds, almond milk, vanilla extract, and honey.
2. Stir well and refrigerate overnight or for at least 4 hours.
3. Before serving, give it a good stir.
4. Top with mixed berries and sliced almonds.
5. Enjoy this cool and satisfying pudding.

NUTRITIONAL INFORMATION:

- Calories: 250 per serving
- Protein: 8g
- Fat: 15g
- Carbohydrates: 25g

Mediterranean Chia Seed Pudding

Serving Size:1

5 minutes
(plus chilling time)

INTRODUCTION

Fuel your day with a nutrient-packed chia seed pudding infused with Mediterranean flavors. This make-ahead breakfast is not only delicious but also a great source of omega-3 fatty acids.

INGREDIENTS

- 3 tbsp chia seeds
- 1cup unsweetened almond milk
- 1/2 tsp vanilla extract
- 1 tbsp honey
- 1/4 cup mixed berries
- Sliced almonds for topping

INSTRUCTIONS

1. In a jar, mix chia seeds, almond milk, vanilla extract, and honey.
2. Stir well and refrigerate overnight or for at least 4 hours.
3. Before serving, give it a good stir.
4. Top with mixed berries and sliced almonds.
5. Enjoy this cool and satisfying pudding.

NUTRITIONAL INFORMATION:

- Calories: 250 per serving
- Protein: 8g
- Fat: 15g
- Carbohydrates: 25g

Mediterranean Shakshuka

INTRODUCTION

Transport yourself to the vibrant streets of the Mediterranean with this Shakshuka—a flavorful combination of poached eggs in a rich tomato and bell pepper sauce.

INGREDIENTS

- 2 eggs
- 1can (14 oz) crushed tomatoes
- 1bell pepper, diced
- 1/2 onion, finely chopped
- 2 cloves garlic, minced
- 1tsp ground cumin
- 1 tsp smoked paprika
- Salt and pepper to taste
- Fresh parsley for garnish

INSTRUCTIONS

1. In a pan, sauté onions and bell peppers until softened.
2. Add minced garlic, ground cumin, and smoked grain bread.paprika. Cook for an additional minute.
3. Pour in the crushed tomatoes and simmer for 10 minutes.
4. Create small wells in the sauce and crack eggs into them.
5. Cover and cook until the eggs are poached to your liking.
6. Season with salt and pepper and garnish with fresh parsley.
7. Serve with crusty whole-

NUTRITIONAL INFORMATION:

- Calories: 300 per serving
- Protein: 15g
- Fat: 15g
- Carbohydrates: 25g

Mediterranean Breakfast Wrap

Serving Size:1   10 minutes

INTRODUCTION

A portable breakfast bursting with Mediterranean flavors. This wrap combines hummus, cucumber, cherry tomatoes, and feta cheese, all wrapped in a whole-grain tortilla.

INGREDIENTS

- 1 whole-grain tortilla
- 2 tbsp hummus
- 1/4 cup cucumber, thinly sliced
- 1/4 cup cherry tomatoes, halved
- 2 tbsp crumbled feta cheese
- Fresh dill for garnish
- Salt and pepper to taste

INSTRUCTIONS

1. Spread hummus evenly on the whole-grain tortilla.
2. Layer cucumber slices and cherry tomatoes on top.
3. prinkle crumbled feta cheese over the vegetables.
4. Season with salt and pepper to taste.
5. Garnish with fresh dill.
6. Roll the tortilla tightly and slice in half.
7. Enjoy this handheld Mediterranean delight

NUTRITIONAL INFORMATION:

- Calories: 280 per serving
- Protein: 10g
- Fat: 12g
- Carbohydrates: 35g

Mediterranean Quinoa Breakfast Bowl

Serving Size:1 20 minutes

INTRODUCTION

A protein-packed breakfast bowl featuring fluffy quinoa, sautéed spinach, roasted cherry tomatoes, and a perfectly poached egg, all drizzled with a lemony tahini dressing.

INGREDIENTS

- 1/2 cup cooked quinoa
- Handful of fresh spinach
- 1/2 cup cherry tomatoes, roasted
- 1 poached egg
- 1 tbsp tahini
- 1 tsp lemon juice
- Salt and pepper to taste
- Chopped parsley for garnish

INSTRUCTIONS

1. Cook quinoa according to package instructions.
2. Sauté fresh spinach until wilted.
3. Roast cherry tomatoes in the oven until slightly caramelized.
4. In a bowl, assemble quinoa, sautéed spinach, and roasted cherry tomatoes.
5. Top with a perfectly poached egg.
6. In a small bowl, mix tahini, lemon juice, salt, and pepper for the dressing.
7. Drizzle the tahini dressing over the bowl and garnish with chopped parsley.
8. Delight in this wholesome and satisfying breakfast bowl.

NUTRITIONAL INFORMATION:

- Calories: 380 per serving
- Protein: 18g
- Fat: 18g
- Carbohydrates: 35g

Mediterranean Fruit Salad

Serving Size:1 10 minutes

INTRODUCTION

A refreshing and vibrant fruit salad featuring a medley of seasonal fruits, drizzled with honey and a hint of mint. Perfect for a light and energizing start to your day.

INGREDIENTS

- 1 cup mixed fruits (watermelon, cantaloupe, pineapple, berries)
- 1 tbsp honey
- Fresh mint leaves for garnish

INSTRUCTIONS

1. Dice watermelon, cantaloupe, pineapple, and any berries of your choice.
2. Mix the fruits in a bowl.
3. Drizzle honey over the fruit mixture.
4. Toss gently to coat the fruits in honey.
5. Garnish with fresh mint leaves.
6. Chill in the refrigerator for a refreshing breakfast.

NUTRITIONAL INFORMATION:

- Calories: 120 per serving
- Protein: 2g
- Fat: 0g
- Carbohydrates: 30g

Mediterranean Pancakes with Yogurt and Pistachios

Serving Size:2 15 minutes

INTRODUCTION

A delightful twist on classic pancakes. These Mediterranean-inspired pancakes are topped with Greek yogurt, fresh berries, and a sprinkle of crushed pistachios.

INGREDIENTS

- 1 cup pancake mix
- 3/4 cup water or milk
- 1/2 cup Greek yogurt
- Mixed berries for topping
- 2 tbsp crushed pistachios
- Maple syrup for drizzling

INSTRUCTIONS

1. Prepare pancakes according to the mix instructions.
2. Stack the pancakes on a plate.
3. Spread a layer of Greek yogurt over the pancakes.
4. Top with mixed berries and crushed pistachios.
5. Drizzle with maple syrup.
6. Enjoy this Mediterranean-inspired pancake delight.

NUTRITIONAL INFORMATION:

- Calories: 280 per serving
- Protein: 8g
- Fat: 10g
- Carbohydrates: 40g

Mediterranean Breakfast Smoothie Bowl

Serving Size:1 10 minutes

INTRODUCTION

Start your day with a vibrant and nutrient-packed smoothie bowl. Blended with spinach, banana, Greek yogurt, and topped with granola and fresh fruit.

INGREDIENTS

- 1 cup fresh spinach
- 1 frozen banana
- 1/2 cup Greek yogurt
- 1/2 cup almond milk
- Toppings: Granola, sliced banana, chia seeds

INSTRUCTIONS

1. In a blender, combine fresh spinach, frozen banana, Greek yogurt, and almond milk.
2. Blend until smooth and creamy.
3. Pour the smoothie into a bowl.
4. Top with granola, sliced banana, and a sprinkle of chia seeds.
5. Dive into this nutritious and delicious breakfast bowl.

NUTRITIONAL INFORMATION:

- Calories: 300 per serving
- Protein: 15g
- Fat: 10g
- carbohydrates: 45g

Mediterranean Egg Muffins

Serving Size:2 15 minutes

INTRODUCTION

Perfect for a quick and portable breakfast, these Mediterranean egg muffins are loaded with spinach, sun-dried tomatoes, feta cheese, and herbs.

INGREDIENTS

- 4 eggs
- 1/2 cup fresh spinach, chopped
- 1/4 cup sun-dried tomatoes, chopped
- 2 tbsp crumbled feta cheese
- 1 tbsp fresh basil, finely chopped
- Salt and pepper to taste

INSTRUCTIONS

1. Preheat the oven to 375°F (190°C) and grease a muffin tin.
2. In a bowl, whisk together eggs, chopped spinach, sun-dried tomatoes, feta cheese, fresh basil, salt, and pepper.
3. Pour the egg mixture evenly into the muffin cups.
4. Bake for 15-20 minutes or until the eggs are set.
5. Allow them to cool slightly before removing from the tin.
6. Enjoy these flavorful and protein-packed egg muffins.

NUTRITIONAL INFORMATION:

- Calories: 180 per serving
- Protein: 14g
- Fat: 12g
- Carbohydrates: 4g

Mediterranean Overnight Oats

Serving Size:2 15 minutes

INTRODUCTION

Simplify your mornings with these delicious overnight oats infused with Mediterranean flavors. Prepare them the night before for a quick and nourishing breakfast.

INGREDIENTS

- 1/2 cup rolled oats
- 1/2 cup Greek yogurt
- 1/2 cup almond milk
- 1 tbsp honey
- 1/4 cup mixed berries
- 1 tbsp sliced almonds

INSTRUCTIONS

1. In a jar or bowl, combine rolled oats, Greek yogurt, almond milk, and honey.
2. Stir well, cover, and refrigerate overnight.
3. In the morning, give it a good stir.
4. Top with mixed berries and sliced almonds.
5. Enjoy these creamy and satisfying overnight oats.

NUTRITIONAL INFORMATION:

- Calories: 300 per serving
- Protein: 15g
- Fat: 10g
- Carbohydrates: 40g

Chapter 6: Lively Lunches

Delicious lunch recipes to get you started on your Mediterranean journey

✹ A Big Thank You for Joining This Tasty Journey! ✾

Hello there,

I really want to thank you for choosing to explore the delicious adventure in the "Mediterranean Diet Cookbook for Seniors." It's not just about getting recipes; it shows your commitment to a healthier and happier life.

Your presence makes this journey rich and exciting. As someone who loves putting passion into each page, I'm so happy you've decided to be part of this adventure.

Now, as we go through these tasty recipes, I invite you to take a moment —share your thoughts and experiences. Your feedback is like a treasure map guiding me to make things even better for those who come after you.

Your voice is important and shapes the story of this cooking adventure. Every word you share can inspire and connect with others who haven't discovered the magic in these pages yet. It's not just a review; it's a gift to others looking for a way to be healthy and happy.

So, could you take a moment to write down your thoughts? Tell me about the flavors you liked, the recipes that became your favorites, and the moments that made you smile. Your words aren't just for me; they help build a community of food lovers, each adding their unique touch to a happy and healthy life.

As you enjoy the good feelings after a tasty meal from this cookbook, know that your words can reach beyond your kitchen. They can inspire others to enjoy every meal and make every day a chance for well-being.

Thank you for more than just picking a cookbook. Thank you for becoming a part of a group of people who love good food and want to live a vibrant life.

With gratitude,

[Dr. Campbell's]
Publisher of the "Mediterranean Diet Cookbook for Seniors"

Mediterranean Chickpea Salad Bowl

Serving Size:2 15 minutes

INTRODUCTION

This vibrant salad bowl is packed with protein and flavor. Chickpeas, cherry tomatoes, cucumbers, and feta cheese are tossed in a lemony herb dressing.

INGREDIENTS

- 1 cup chickpeas, cooked
- 1 cup cherry tomatoes, halved
- 1 cucumber, diced
- 2 tbsp feta cheese, crumbled
- Fresh parsley for garnish
- Dressing: Olive oil, lemon juice, oregano, salt, and pepper

INSTRUCTIONS

1. In a bowl, combine chickpeas, cherry tomatoes, and cucumber.
2. Sprinkle crumbled feta cheese over the salad.
3. In a small jar, mix olive oil, lemon juice, oregano, salt, and pepper for the dressing.
4. Drizzle the dressing over the salad.
5. Toss well and garnish with fresh parsley.
6. Serve this refreshing chickpea salad.

NUTRITIONAL INFORMATION:

- Calories: 280 per serving
- Protein: 12g
- Fat: 14g
- Carbohydrates: 30g

Mediterranean Quinoa Stuffed Peppers

Serving Size:4 30 minutes

INTRODUCTION

These colorful stuffed peppers are filled with a mixture of quinoa, black olives, cherry tomatoes, and feta cheese, creating a wholesome and satisfying lunch.

INGREDIENTS

- 4 bell peppers, halved
- 1 cup cooked quinoa
- 1/4 cup black olives, sliced
- 1/2 cup cherry tomatoes, diced
- 2 tbsp feta cheese, crumbled
- Fresh basil for garnish
- Olive oil for drizzling

INSTRUCTIONS

1. Preheat the oven to 375°F (190°C).
2. Place bell pepper halves in a baking dish.
3. In a bowl, mix cooked quinoa, black olives, cherry tomatoes, and feta cheese.
4. Spoon the quinoa mixture into the pepper halves.
5. Drizzle with olive oil.
6. Bake until the peppers are tender.
7. Garnish with fresh basil and serve these Mediterranean stuffed peppers.

NUTRITIONAL INFORMATION:

- Calories: 220 per serving
- Protein: 10g
- Fat: 12g
- Carbohydrates: 25g

Mediterranean Grilled Chicken Salad

 Serving Size:1

 20 minutes

INTRODUCTION

A hearty and protein-packed grilled chicken salad featuring mixed greens, cherry tomatoes, Kalamata olives, and a zesty lemon vinaigrette.

INGREDIENTS

- 1 grilled chicken breast, sliced
- Mixed greens
- 1/2 cup cherry tomatoes, halved
- 1/4 cup Kalamata olives, sliced
- Feta cheese for topping
- Dressing: Olive oil, lemon juice, garlic, oregano, salt, and pepper

INSTRUCTIONS

1. Arrange mixed greens on a plate.
2. Top with grilled chicken slices, cherry tomatoes, and Kalamata olives.
3. Sprinkle crumbled feta cheese over the salad.
4. In a small bowl, whisk together olive oil, lemon juice, minced garlic, oregano, salt, and pepper for the dressing.
5. Drizzle the dressing over the salad.
6. Toss gently and enjoy this satisfying grilled chicken salad.

NUTRITIONAL INFORMATION:

- Calories: 350 per serving
- Protein: 25g
- Fat: 18g
- Carbohydrates: 20g

Mediterranean Vegetable Wrap

Serving Size:1 15 minutes

INTRODUCTION

Wrap up the goodness of the Mediterranean with this vegetable-packed wrap. Hummus, roasted vegetables, feta cheese, and a sprinkle of fresh herbs create a delightful lunch option.

INGREDIENTS

- 1whole-grain wrap
- 2 tbsp hummus
- Assorted roasted vegetables (zucchini, bell peppers, eggplant)
- 2 tbsp feta cheese, crumbled
- Fresh mint for garnish

INSTRUCTIONS

1. Spread hummus evenly on the whole-grain wrap.
2. Arrange roasted vegetables on the wrap.
3. Sprinkle crumbled feta cheese over the vegetables.
4. Garnish with fresh mint.
5. Roll the wrap tightly and slice in half.
6. Enjoy this flavorful and nutritious Mediterranean vegetable wrap.

NUTRITIONAL INFORMATION:

- Calories: 280 per serving
- Protein: 10g
- Fat: 12g
- Carbohydrates: 35g

Mediterranean Shrimp and Couscous Bowl

Serving Size:2 25 minutes

INTRODUCTION

Indulge in a seafood delight with this Mediterranean shrimp and couscous bowl. Succulent shrimp, fluffy couscous, cherry tomatoes, and feta cheese come together in a symphony of flavors.

INGREDIENTS

- 1 cup cooked couscous
- 1/2 lb shrimp, peeled and deveined
- 1/2 cup cherry tomatoes, halved
- 2 tbsp feta cheese, crumbled
- Fresh parsley for garnish
- Dressing: Olive oil, lemon juice, garlic, oregano, salt, and pepper

INSTRUCTIONS

1. Cook couscous according to package instructions.
2. In a pan, sauté shrimp until cooked.
3. In a bowl, combine cooked couscous, sautéed shrimp, cherry tomatoes, and feta cheese.
4. In a small jar, whisk together olive oil, lemon juice, minced garlic, oregano, salt, and pepper for the dressing.
5. Drizzle the dressing over the bowl.
6. Garnish with fresh parsley and enjoy this Mediterranean shrimp and couscous bowl.

NUTRITIONAL INFORMATION:

- Calories: 300 per serving
- Protein: 20g
- Fat: 12g
- Carbohydrates: 30g

Mediterranean Eggplant and Lentil Sala

Serving Size:2 30 minutes

INTRODUCTION

This hearty salad combines roasted eggplant, cooked lentils, cherry tomatoes, and crumbled feta cheese, all tossed in a balsamic vinaigrette.

INGREDIENTS

- 1 medium eggplant, diced
- 1 cup cooked lentils
- 1/2 cup cherry tomatoes, halved
- 2 tbsp feta cheese, crumbled
- Fresh basil for garnish
- Dressing: Balsamic vinegar, olive oil, garlic, salt, and pepper

INSTRUCTIONS

1. Preheat the oven to 400°F (200°C).
2. 2. Roast diced eggplant until golden brown.
3. In a bowl, mix roasted eggplant, cooked lentils, cherry tomatoes, and crumbled feta cheese.
4. In a small bowl, whisk together balsamic vinegar, olive oil, minced garlic, salt, and pepper for the dressing.
5. Drizzle the dressing over the salad.
6. Garnish with fresh basil and savor this Mediterranean eggplant and lentil salad.

NUTRITIONAL INFORMATION:

- Calories: 250 per serving
- Protein: 15g
- Fat: 10g
- Carbohydrates: 30g

Mediterranean Turkey and Avocado Wrap

Serving Size:1 15 minutes

INTRODUCTION

A protein-packed wrap featuring lean turkey, creamy avocado, cherry tomatoes, and a zesty yogurt dressing. This Mediterranean-inspired wrap is both nutritious and delicious.

INGREDIENTS

- 1 whole-grain wrap
- 3 oz sliced turkey breast
- 1/2 avocado, sliced
- 1/4 cup cherry tomatoes, halved
- Yogurt dressing: Greek yogurt, lemon juice, dill, salt, and pepper

INSTRUCTIONS

1. Lay the whole-grain wrap on a flat surface.
2. Arrange sliced turkey, avocado, and cherry tomatoes on the wrap.
3. In a small bowl, mix Greek yogurt, lemon juice, chopped dill, salt, and pepper for the dressing.
4. Drizzle the dressing over the ingredients.
5. Roll the wrap tightly and slice in half.
6. Enjoy this satisfying and flavorful Mediterranean turkey and avocado wrap.

NUTRITIONAL INFORMATION:

- Calories: 320 per serving
- Protein: 25g
- Fat: 15g
- Carbohydrates: 20g

Mediterranean Salmon and Orzo Bowl

Serving Size:1 25 minutes

INTRODUCTION

This wholesome bowl combines flaky salmon, orzo pasta, cherry tomatoes, and a lemony herb dressing. It's a delightful blend of textures and flavors for a fulfilling lunch.

INGREDIENTS

- 1 fillet salmon, grilled and flaked
- 1/2 cup cooked orzo pasta
- 1/2 cup cherry tomatoes, halved
- 2 tbsp feta cheese, crumbled
- Fresh dill for garnish
- Dressing: Olive oil, lemon juice, oregano, salt, and pepper

INSTRUCTIONS

1. Grill the salmon fillet until flaky.
2. Cook orzo pasta according to package instructions.
3. In a bowl, combine flaked salmon, cooked orzo, cherry tomatoes, and crumbled feta cheese.
4. In a small jar, whisk together olive oil, lemon juice, oregano, salt, and pepper for the dressing.
5. Drizzle the dressing over the bowl.
6. Garnish with fresh dill and enjoy this Mediterranean salmon and orzo bowl.

NUTRITIONAL INFORMATION:

- Calories: 350 per serving
- Protein: 22g
- Fat: 18g
- Carbohydrates: 25g

Mediterranean Falafel Bowl

Serving Size:2 20 minutes

INTRODUCTION

Savor the flavors of the Mediterranean with this falafel bowl. Crispy falafel, quinoa, cucumber, and a tahini dressing create a satisfying and nutritious lunch.

INGREDIENTS

- 4 falafel patties, cooked
- 1cup cooked quinoa
- 1 cucumber, diced
- 2 tbsp hummus
- Tahini dressing: Tahini, lemon juice, garlic, salt, and pepper

INSTRUCTIONS

1. Cook falafel patties according to package instructions.
2. In a bowl, combine cooked quinoa, diced cucumber, and falafel patties.
3. Add dollops of hummus to the bowl.
4. In a small bowl, whisk together tahini, lemon juice, minced garlic, salt, and pepper for the dressing.
5. Drizzle the dressing over the bowl.
6. Toss gently and enjoy this flavorful and protein-rich Mediterranean falafel bowl.

NUTRITIONAL INFORMATION:

- Calories: 300 per serving
- Protein: 14g
- Fat: 15g
- Carbohydrates: 30g

Mediterranean Caprese Salad

Serving Size:1 10 minutes

INTRODUCTION

A classic Caprese salad gets a Mediterranean twist with the addition of Kalamata olives and a balsamic glaze. Fresh mozzarella, cherry tomatoes, and basil create a simple and delightful lunch.

INGREDIENTS

- 1 cup cherry tomatoes, halved
- 1 cup fresh mozzarella balls
- 1/4 cup Kalamata olives, sliced
- Fresh basil leaves
- Balsamic glaze for drizzling
- Olive oil for drizzling
- Salt and pepper to taste

INSTRUCTIONS

1. Arrange cherry tomatoes, fresh mozzarella balls, and Kalamata olives on a plate.
2. Tuck fresh basil leaves among the ingredients.
3. Drizzle with balsamic glaze and olive oil.
4. Season with salt and pepper to taste.
5. Enjoy this light and refreshing Mediterranean Caprese salad.

NUTRITIONAL INFORMATION:

- Calories: 250 per serving
- Protein: 12g
- Fat: 18g
- Carbohydrates: 15g

Mediterranean Pesto Chicken Pasta

Serving Size:2 | 25 minutes

INTRODUCTION

Indulge in a pasta dish that combines the richness of pesto with grilled chicken, cherry tomatoes, and pine nuts. This Mediterranean-inspired recipe is a celebration of flavors.

INGREDIENTS

- 8 oz whole-grain pasta
- 1 grilled chicken breast, sliced
- 1 cup cherry tomatoes, halved
- 2 tbsp pine nuts, toasted
- Pesto sauce: Fresh basil, garlic, pine nuts, Parmesan cheese, olive oil, salt, and pepper

INSTRUCTIONS

1. Cook whole-grain pasta according to package instructions.
2. In a blender, combine fresh basil, garlic, pine nuts, Parmesan cheese, olive oil, salt, and pepper to make the pesto sauce.
3. Toss the cooked pasta with sliced grilled chicken, cherry tomatoes, and toasted pine nuts.
4. Drizzle the pesto sauce over the pasta and toss until well coated.
5. Serve this savory and aromatic Mediterranean pesto chicken pasta.

NUTRITIONAL INFORMATION:

- Calories: 350 per serving
- Protein: 20g
- Fat: 15g
- Carbohydrates: 35g

Mediterranean Lentil Soup

Serving Size:4 40 minutes

INTRODUCTION

Warm up your lunchtime with a hearty Mediterranean lentil soup. Packed with lentils, vegetables, and aromatic herbs, this soup is both comforting and nutritious.

INGREDIENTS

- 1cup dry lentils, rinsed
- 1 onion, diced
- 2 carrots, diced
- 2celery stalks, diced
- 3cloves garlic, minced
- 1 can (14 oz) diced tomatoes
- 6cups vegetable broth
- 1 tsp cumin
- 1tsp smoked paprika
- Fresh parsley for garnish
- Salt and pepper to taste

INSTRUCTIONS

1. In a large pot, sauté diced onion, carrots, and celery until softened.
2. Add minced garlic, cumin, and smoked paprika, and cook for an additional minute.
3. Pour in vegetable broth, diced tomatoes, and rinsed lentils.
4. Bring the soup to a boil, then reduce heat and simmer until lentils are tender.
5. Season with salt and pepper to taste.
6. Garnish with fresh parsley and enjoy this wholesome Mediterranean lentil soup.

NUTRITIONAL INFORMATION:

- Calories: 250 per serving
- Protein: 15g
- Fat: 2g
- Carbohydrates: 45g

Chapter 7: Satisfying Snacks

Delicious Mediterranean-inspired snack recipes to satisfy your cravings

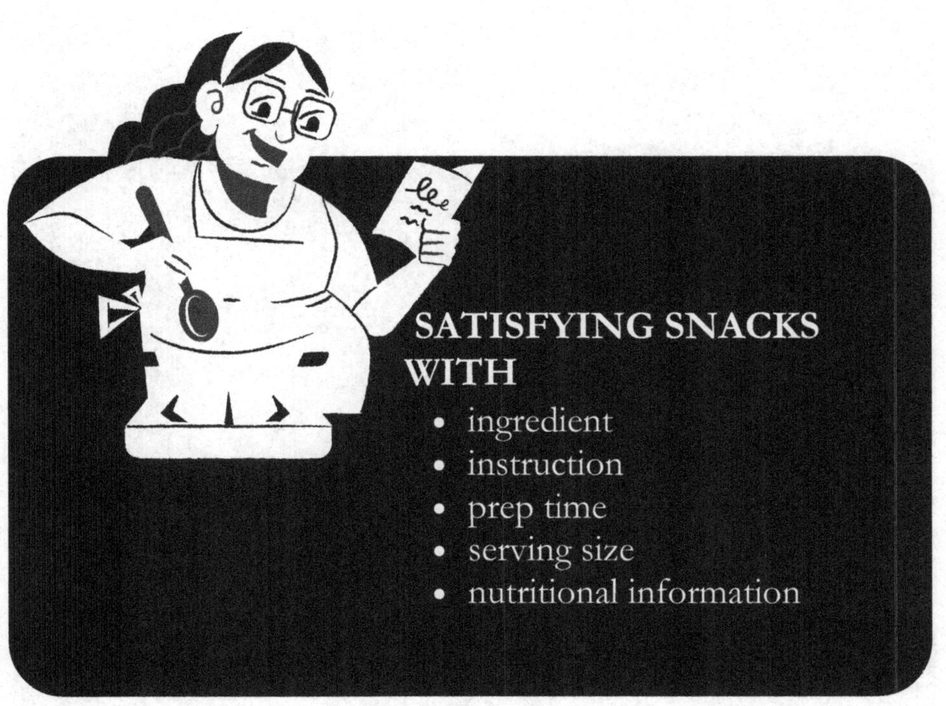

Mediterranean Hummus Platter

Serving Size:4 15 minutes

INTRODUCTION

Elevate your snacking experience with a vibrant hummus platter featuring various Mediterranean delights. Perfect for sharing or enjoying solo.

INGREDIENTS

- Hummus
- Cherry tomatoes
- Cucumber slices
- Kalamata olives
- Feta cheese
- Pita wedges

INSTRUCTIONS

1. Arrange hummus in the center of a platter.
2. with cherry tomatoes, cucumber slices, Kalamata olives, and crumbled feta cheese.
3. Serve with pita wedges for dipping.
4. Enjoy this delightful Mediterranean hummus platter.

NUTRITIONAL INFORMATION:

- Calories: 200 per serving
- Protein: 8g
- Fat: 12g
- Carbohydrates: 18g

Greek Yogurt and Honey Parfait

 Serving Size:1  10 minutes

INTRODUCTION

Indulge in a sweet and creamy Greek yogurt parfait drizzled with honey and topped with fresh fruits and nuts.

INGREDIENTS

- Greek yogurt
- Honey
- Fresh berries (strawberries, blueberries)
- Almonds, chopped

INSTRUCTIONS

1. In a glass, layer Greek yogurt and fresh berries.
2. Drizzle honey over each layer.
3. Top with chopped almonds.
4. Repeat layers.
5. Enjoy this luscious Greek yogurt and honey parfait.

NUTRITIONAL INFORMATION:

- Calories: 250 per serving
- Protein: 15g
- Fat: 10g
- Carbohydrates: 25g

Mediterranean Stuffed Grape Leaves

Serving Size:6 20 minutes

INTRODUCTION

Indulge in a sweet and creamy Greek yogurt parfait drizzled with honey and topped with fresh fruits and nuts.

INGREDIENTS

- Grape leaves
- Rice, cooked
- Pine nuts
- Fresh dill, chopped
- Lemon juice
- Olive oil

INSTRUCTIONS

1. Mix cooked rice, pine nuts, chopped fresh dill, lemon juice, and a drizzle of olive oil.
2. Place a spoonful of the mixture onto a grape leaf and roll.
3. Serve as a delightful Mediterranean stuffed grape leaves snack.

NUTRITIONAL INFORMATION:

- Calories: 180 per serving
- Protein: 4g
- Fat: 8g
- Carbohydrates: 25g

Mediterranean Olive Tapenade

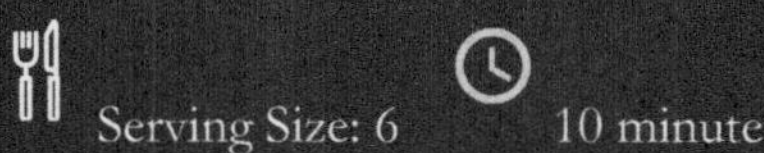

INTRODUCTION

Dive into the bold flavors of olive tapenade, a spread made with Kalamata olives, capers, garlic, and olive oil. Perfect with crackers or sliced baguette.

INGREDIENTS

- Kalamata olives, pitted
- Capers
- Garlic, minced
- Olive oil
- Lemon juice
- Fresh parsley, chopped

INSTRUCTIONS

1. In a food processor, blend pitted Kalamata olives, capers, minced garlic, olive oil, lemon juice, and fresh parsley until smooth.
2. Serve this flavorful Mediterranean olive tapenade with crackers or sliced baguette.

NUTRITIONAL INFORMATION:

- Calories: 90 per serving
- Protein: 1g
- Fat: 8g
- Carbohydrates: 4g

Mediterranean Vegetable Skewers

Serving Size:6 20 minutes

INTRODUCTION

Enjoy a colorful and flavorful snack with Mediterranean vegetable skewers, grilled to perfection and served with a yogurt-based dipping sauce.

INGREDIENTS

- Cherry tomatoes
- Bell peppers, cut into chunks
- Red onion, cut into wedges
- Zucchini, sliced
- Olive oil
- Greek yogurt
- Garlic, minced
- Lemon juice
- Oregano

INSTRUCTIONS

1. Thread cherry tomatoes, bell peppers, red onion, and zucchini onto skewers.
2. Brush with olive oil and grill until vegetables are tender.
3. Mix Greek yogurt, minced garlic, lemon juice, and oregano for the dipping sauce.
4. Serve these Mediterranean vegetable skewers with the yogurt sauce.

NUTRITIONAL INFORMATION:

- Calories: 120 per serving
- Protein: 3g
- Fat: 8g
- Carbohydrates: 10g

Mediterranean Olive Tapenade

Serving Size: 6 10 minutes

INTRODUCTION

Dive into the bold flavors of olive tapenade, a spread made with Kalamata olives, capers, garlic, and olive oil. Perfect with crackers or sliced baguette.

INGREDIENTS

- Kalamata olives, pitted
- Capers
- Garlic, minced
- Olive oil
- Lemon juice
- Fresh parsley, chopped

INSTRUCTIONS

1. In a food processor, blend pitted Kalamata olives, capers, minced garlic, olive oil, lemon juice, and fresh parsley until smooth.
2. Serve this flavorful Mediterranean olive tapenade with crackers or sliced baguette.

NUTRITIONAL INFORMATION:

- Calories: 90 per serving
- Protein: 1g
- Fat: 8g
- Carbohydrates: 4g

Mediterranean Eggplant Dip (Baba Ganoush)

Serving Size: 6 40 minutes

INTRODUCTION

Experience the smoky and rich flavors of Baba Ganoush, a Mediterranean eggplant dip. Perfect for dipping veggies or pita.

INGREDIENTS

- Eggplant
- Tahini
- Garlic, minced
- Lemon juice
- Olive oil
- Fresh parsley, chopped

INSTRUCTIONS

1. Roast or grill the eggplant until the skin is charred and the flesh is soft.
2. Scoop out the eggplant flesh and blend with tahini, minced garlic, lemon juice, and olive oil until smooth.
3. Garnish with chopped fresh parsley.
4. Serve this creamy Mediterranean eggplant dip with your favorite dippers.

NUTRITIONAL INFORMATION:

- Calories: 120 per serving
- Protein: 2g
- Fat: 10g
- Carbohydrates: 8g

Mediterranean Tomato Bruschetta

 Serving Size: 4 20 minutes

INTRODUCTION

Delight in the freshness of tomato bruschetta, a classic Mediterranean appetizer with diced tomatoes, garlic, basil, and a drizzle of balsamic glaze.

INGREDIENTS

- Baguette, sliced
- Tomatoes, diced
- Garlic, minced
- Fresh basil, chopped
- Balsamic glaze
- Olive oil

INSTRUCTIONS

1. Toast baguette slices.
2. In a bowl, mix diced tomatoes, minced garlic, chopped fresh basil, and a drizzle of olive oil.
3. Spoon the tomato mixture onto the baguette slices.
4. Finish with a drizzle of balsamic glaze.
5. Enjoy this simple and tasty Mediterranean tomato bruschetta.

NUTRITIONAL INFORMATION:

- Calories: 110 per serving
- Protein: 3g
- Fat: 4g
- Carbohydrates: 15g

Mediterranean Cucumber Bites

 Serving Size: 4 15 minutes

INTRODUCTION

Experience a refreshing snack with Mediterranean cucumber bites filled with a blend of tzatziki, cherry tomatoes, and fresh herbs.

INGREDIENTS

- English cucumber, sliced
- Tzatziki sauce
- Cherry tomatoes, halved
- Fresh dill, chopped

INSTRUCTIONS

1. Top cucumber slices with a dollop of tzatziki sauce.
2. Place a halved cherry tomato on top.
3. Garnish with chopped fresh dill.
4. Enjoy these light and flavorful Mediterranean cucumber bites.

NUTRITIONAL INFORMATION:

- Calories: 80 per serving
- Protein: 2g
- Fat: 5g
- Carbohydrates: 8g

Mediterranean Roasted Red Pepper Hummus

Serving Size: 6 15 minutes

INTRODUCTION

Dive into the rich flavors of roasted red pepper hummus, a delightful spread made with chickpeas, tahini, and roasted red peppers.

INGREDIENTS

- Chickpeas, canned and rinsed
- Roasted red peppers, jarred
- Tahini
- Garlic, minced
- Lemon juice
- Olive oil
- Paprika for garnish

INSTRUCTIONS

1. In a food processor, blend chickpeas, roasted red peppers, tahini, minced garlic, lemon juice, and olive oil until smooth.
2. Garnish with a sprinkle of paprika.
3. Serve this Mediterranean roasted red pepper hummus with pita chips or veggie sticks.

NUTRITIONAL INFORMATION:

- Calories: 100 per serving
- Protein: 3g
- Fat: 7g
- Carbohydrates: 10g

Mediterranean Roasted Red Pepper Hummus

Serving Size: 4 15 minutes

INTRODUCTION

Dive into the rich flavors of roasted red pepper hummus, a delightful spread made with chickpeas, tahini, and roasted red peppers.

INGREDIENTS

- Baguette, sliced
- Ripe avocados, mashed
- Feta cheese, crumbled
- Cherry tomatoes, diced
- Balsamic glaze
- Fresh basil, chopped

INSTRUCTIONS

1. Toast baguette slices.
2. Spread mashed avocado on each slice.
3. with crumbled feta, diced cherry tomatoes, and chopped fresh basil.
4. Drizzle with balsamic glaze.
5. Enjoy this flavorful Mediterranean avocado and feta bruschetta.

NUTRITIONAL INFORMATION:

- Calories: 130 per serving
- Protein: 4g
- Fat: 8g
- Carbohydrates: 12g

Mediterranean Quinoa-Stuffed Peppers

Serving Size: 4 25 minutes

INTRODUCTION

Savor the wholesome goodness of quinoa-stuffed mini peppers. These bite-sized snacks are filled with a Mediterranean quinoa blend.

INGREDIENTS

- Mini bell peppers, halved
- Quinoa, cooked
- Feta cheese, crumbled
- Cherry tomatoes, diced
- Kalamata olives, sliced
- Fresh parsley, chopped

INSTRUCTIONS

1. Preheat the oven to 375°F (190°C).
2. Arrange halved mini peppers on a baking sheet.
3. Mix cooked quinoa, crumbled feta, diced cherry tomatoes, sliced Kalamata olives, and chopped fresh parsley.
4. Spoon the quinoa mixture into each pepper half.
5. Bake until peppers are tender.
6. Enjoy these Mediterranean quinoa-stuffed peppers as a delightful snack.

NUTRITIONAL INFORMATION:

- Calories: 160 per serving
- Protein: 6g
- Fat: 8g
- Carbohydrates: 18g

✸ A Big Thank You for Joining This Tasty Journey! ✿

Hello there,

I really want to thank you for choosing to explore the delicious adventure in the "Mediterranean Diet Cookbook for Seniors." It's not just about getting recipes; it shows your commitment to a healthier and happier life.

Your presence makes this journey rich and exciting. As someone who loves putting passion into each page, I'm so happy you've decided to be part of this adventure.

Now, as we go through these tasty recipes, I invite you to take a moment —share your thoughts and experiences. Your feedback is like a treasure map guiding me to make things even better for those who come after you.

Your voice is important and shapes the story of this cooking adventure. Every word you share can inspire and connect with others who haven't discovered the magic in these pages yet. It's not just a review; it's a gift to others looking for a way to be healthy and happy.

So, could you take a moment to write down your thoughts? Tell me about the flavors you liked, the recipes that became your favorites, and the moments that made you smile. Your words aren't just for me; they help build a community of food lovers, each adding their unique touch to a happy and healthy life.

As you enjoy the good feelings after a tasty meal from this cookbook, know that your words can reach beyond your kitchen. They can inspire others to enjoy every meal and make every day a chance for well-being.

Thank you for more than just picking a cookbook. Thank you for becoming a part of a group of people who love good food and want to live a vibrant life.

With gratitude,

[Dr. Campbell's] ★★★★★
Publisher of the "Mediterranean Diet Cookbook for Seniors"

Chapter 8: Delectable Dinners

Here are delectable dinner recipes from the Mediterranean diet, each offering a unique blend of flavors and nutrients:

Grilled Lemon Herb Chicken Skewers

Serving Size: 4 40 minutes

INTRODUCTION

Savor the succulence of grilled lemon herb chicken skewers, a perfect blend of Mediterranean flavors that will delight your taste buds.

INGREDIENTS

- Chicken breast, cubed
- Lemon juice
- Olive oil
- Garlic, minced
- Fresh rosemary, chopped
- Salt and pepper

INSTRUCTIONS

1. In a bowl, mix lemon juice, olive oil, minced garlic, chopped rosemary, salt, and pepper.
2. Marinate chicken cubes in the mixture for at least 30 minutes.
3. Thread onto skewers and grill until fully cooked.
4. Serve with your favorite Mediterranean sides.

NUTRITIONAL INFORMATION:

- Calories: 250 per serving
- Protein: 30g
- Fat: 12g
- Carbohydrates: 5g

Mediterranean Stuffed Bell Peppers

Serving Size: 4 45 minutes

INTRODUCTION

Enjoy a wholesome dinner with Mediterranean stuffed bell peppers filled with a delightful mixture of quinoa, tomatoes, olives, and feta cheese.

INGREDIENTS

- Bell peppers, halved
- Quinoa, cooked
- Cherry tomatoes, diced
- Kalamata olives, sliced
- Feta cheese, crumbled
- Olive oil
- Fresh oregano, chopped

INSTRUCTIONS

1. Preheat the oven to 375°F (190°C).
2. Mix cooked quinoa, diced tomatoes, sliced olives, crumbled feta, olive oil, and chopped oregano.
3. Fill each bell pepper half with the quinoa mixture.
4. Bake until peppers are tender.
5. Serve these Mediterranean stuffed bell peppers with a side salad.

NUTRITIONAL INFORMATION:

- Calories: 300 per serving
- Protein: 12g
- Fat: 15g
- Carbohydrates: 30g

Lemon Garlic Shrimp Pasta

Serving Size: 4 25 minutes

INTRODUCTION

Indulge in the citrusy goodness of lemon garlic shrimp pasta, a quick and flavorful Mediterranean dish that combines shrimp, pasta, and vibrant herbs.

INGREDIENTS

- Shrimp, peeled and deveined
- Linguine pasta
- Lemon zest
- Garlic, minced
- Cherry tomatoes, halved
- Fresh parsley, chopped
- Olive oil

INSTRUCTIONS

1. Cook linguine pasta according to package instructions.
2. In a pan, sauté shrimp with olive oil, minced garlic, and lemon zest until shrimp are pink.
3. Toss in cooked pasta, cherry tomatoes, and chopped parsley.
4. Serve immediately and enjoy this zesty Mediterranean pasta.

NUTRITIONAL INFORMATION:

- Calories: 350 per serving
- Protein: 20g
- Fat: 10g
- Carbohydrates: 45g

Mediterranean Vegetable Couscous Bowl

 Serving Size: 4  30 minutes

INTRODUCTION

Create a vibrant and nutrient-packed dinner with a Mediterranean vegetable couscous bowl, featuring roasted veggies, fluffy couscous, and a zesty tahini dressing.

INGREDIENTS

- Couscous, cooked
- Zucchini, diced
- Cherry tomatoes, halved
- Red onion, sliced
- Chickpeas, cooked
- Tahini
- Lemon juice
- Fresh mint, chopped

INSTRUCTIONS

1. Roast zucchini, cherry tomatoes, and red onion in the oven.
2. Mix cooked couscous and chickpeas.
3. Combine roasted vegetables with the couscous mixture.
4. Drizzle with a dressing made from tahini, lemon juice, and chopped fresh mint.
5. Enjoy this wholesome Mediterranean vegetable couscous bowl.

NUTRITIONAL INFORMATION:

- Calories: 280 per serving
- Protein: 10g
- Fat: 8g
- Carbohydrates: 45g

Greek Lamb Gyro Wrap

 Serving Size: 2   20 minutes

INTRODUCTION

Experience the bold flavors of a Greek lamb gyro wrap, featuring succulent lamb, tzatziki sauce, and crisp veggies wrapped in warm pita bread.

INGREDIENTS

- Lamb slices, cooked
- Pita bread
- Tzatziki sauce
- Tomato, thinly sliced
- Red onion, thinly sliced
- Fresh lettuce

INSTRUCTIONS

1. Warm pita bread in a skillet or microwave.
2. Layer lamb slices, tzatziki sauce, tomato slices, red onion, and lettuce on the pita.
3. Fold into a wrap and secure with toothpicks.
4. Serve this Greek lamb gyro wrap with a side of olives.

NUTRITIONAL INFORMATION:

- Calories: 400 per serving
- Protein: 25g
- Fat: 15g
- Carbohydrates: 40g

Mediterranean Baked Eggplant Parmesan

Serving Size: 4 50 minutes

INTRODUCTION

Delight in the wholesome flavors of Mediterranean baked eggplant parmesan, a comforting dish that layers baked eggplant with marinara sauce and melted mozzarella.

INGREDIENTS

- Eggplant, sliced
- Marinara sauce
- Mozzarella cheese, shredded
- Parmesan cheese, grated
- Fresh basil, chopped

INSTRUCTIONS

1. Preheat the oven to 375°F (190°C).
2. Layer sliced eggplant in a baking dish, alternating with marinara sauce and mozzarella.
3. Repeat the layers and finish with a sprinkle of parmesan.
4. Bake until bubbly and golden.
5. Garnish with chopped fresh basil and enjoy this Mediterranean twist on a classic.

NUTRITIONAL INFORMATION:

- Calories: 320 per serving
- Protein: 15g
- Fat: 18g
- Carbohydrates: 25g

Mediterranean Lemon Herb Salmon

Serving Size: 4  30 minutes

INTRODUCTION

Savor the richness of Mediterranean lemon herb salmon, a delightful dish that combines flaky salmon with a zesty lemon and herb marinade.

INGREDIENTS

- Salmon fillets
- Lemon juice
- Fresh thyme, chopped
- Rosemary, minced
- Garlic, minced
- Olive oil
- Salt and pepper

INSTRUCTIONS

1. Preheat the oven to 400°F (200°C).
2. Mix lemon juice, chopped thyme, minced rosemary, minced garlic, olive oil, salt, and pepper.
3. Marinate salmon fillets in the mixture.
4. Bake until salmon is cooked through.
5. Serve with a side of roasted vegetables for a complete Mediterranean meal.

NUTRITIONAL INFORMATION:

- Calories: 280 per serving
- Protein: 25g
- Fat: 16g
- Carbohydrates: 2g

Mediterranean Quinoa Salad with Roasted Vegetables

Serving Size: 4 25 minutes

INTRODUCTION

Embrace the goodness of a Mediterranean quinoa salad with roasted vegetables, a vibrant and nutritious dish that combines fluffy quinoa with a rainbow of veggies.

INGREDIENTS

- Quinoa, cooked
- Bell peppers, diced
- Cherry tomatoes, halved
- Red onion, thinly sliced
- Cucumber, diced
- Feta cheese, crumbled
- Kalamata olives, sliced
- Greek dressing

INSTRUCTIONS

1. Combine cooked quinoa with diced bell peppers, halved cherry tomatoes, sliced red onion, diced cucumber, crumbled feta, and sliced Kalamata olives.
2. Drizzle with Greek dressing and toss to combine.
3. Chill before serving and relish this refreshing Mediterranean quinoa salad.

NUTRITIONAL INFORMATION:

- Calories: 280 per serving
- Protein: 10g
- Fat: 12g
- Carbohydrates: 35g

Mediterranean Chickpea and Spinach Stew

Serving Size: 4 35 minutes

INTRODUCTION

Warm your soul with a hearty Mediterranean chickpea and spinach stew, a flavorful blend of chickpeas, tomatoes, spinach, and aromatic spices.

INGREDIENTS

- Chickpeas, cooked
- Spinach, chopped
- Tomatoes, diced
- Onion, diced
- Garlic, minced
- Cumin, paprika, and coriander
- Vegetable broth

INSTRUCTIONS

1. In a pot, sauté diced onion and minced garlic until softened.
2. Add diced tomatoes, cooked chickpeas, chopped spinach, cumin, paprika, and coriander.
3. Pour in vegetable broth and simmer until flavors meld.
4. Serve this Mediterranean chickpea and spinach stew with crusty bread.

NUTRITIONAL INFORMATION:

- Calories: 220 per serving
- Protein: 10g
- Fat: 5g
- Carbohydrates: 35g

Mediterranean Ratatouille

 Serving Size: 4 45 minutes

INTRODUCTION

Transport yourself to the Mediterranean with a delightful ratatouille, a vegetable medley featuring eggplant, zucchini, bell peppers, and tomatoes.

INGREDIENTS

- Eggplant, sliced
- Zucchini, sliced
- Bell peppers, sliced
- Tomatoes, sliced
- Garlic, minced
- Fresh thyme and oregano
- Olive oil
- Salt and pepper

INSTRUCTIONS

1. Preheat the oven to 375°F (190°C).
2. Arrange sliced eggplant, zucchini, bell peppers, and tomatoes in a baking dish.
3. Sprinkle minced garlic, fresh thyme, and oregano over the vegetables.
4. Drizzle with olive oil and season with salt and pepper.
5. Bake until vegetables are tender.
6. Serve this Mediterranean ratatouille as a side or a main dish.

NUTRITIONAL INFORMATION:

- Calories: 180 per serving
- Protein: 5g
- Fat: 10g
- Carbohydrates: 25g

Mediterranean Baked Cod with Tomato and Olives

Serving Size: 4 30 minutes

INTRODUCTION

Elevate your dinner experience with Mediterranean baked cod featuring a burst of flavors from ripe tomatoes, Kalamata olives, and aromatic herbs.

INGREDIENTS

- Cod fillets
- Ripe tomatoes, diced
- Kalamata olives, sliced
- Capers
- Garlic, minced
- Fresh parsley, chopped
- Lemon zest
- Olive oil
- Salt and pepper

INSTRUCTIONS

1. Preheat the oven to 375°F (190°C).
2. Place cod fillets in a baking dish.
3. Mix diced tomatoes, sliced olives, capers, minced garlic, chopped parsley, lemon zest, and olive oil.
4. Spoon the mixture over the cod fillets.
5. Bake until the fish is flaky and cooked through.
6. Serve this Mediterranean baked cod over a bed of couscous or quinoa.

NUTRITIONAL INFORMATION:

- Calories: 220 per serving
- Protein: 25g
- Fat: 8g
- Carbohydrates: 10g

Mediterranean Lentil and Vegetable Stuffed Peppers

Serving Size: 4 40 minutes

INTRODUCTION

Indulge in a protein-packed dinner with Mediterranean lentil and vegetable stuffed peppers, a savory blend of lentils, veggies, and aromatic spices.

INGREDIENTS

- Bell peppers, halved
- Lentils, cooked
- Zucchini, diced
- Carrots, grated
- Onion, diced
- Tomato sauce
- Cumin, coriander, and smoked paprika
- Fresh cilantro, chopped

INSTRUCTIONS

1. Preheat the oven to 375°F (190°C).
2. In a bowl, mix cooked lentils, diced zucchini, grated carrots, diced onion, tomato sauce, cumin, coriander, and smoked paprika.
3. Fill each bell pepper half with the lentil mixture.
4. Bake until peppers are tender.
5. Garnish with chopped fresh cilantro and enjoy this Mediterranean twist on stuffed peppers.

NUTRITIONAL INFORMATION:

- Calories: 280 per serving
- Protein: 15g
- Fat: 5g
- Carbohydrates: 45g

✸ A Big Thank You for Joining This Tasty Journey! ✸

Hello there,

I really want to thank you for choosing to explore the delicious adventure in the "Mediterranean Diet Cookbook for Seniors." It's not just about getting recipes; it shows your commitment to a healthier and happier life.

Your presence makes this journey rich and exciting. As someone who loves putting passion into each page, I'm so happy you've decided to be part of this adventure.

Now, as we go through these tasty recipes, I invite you to take a moment —share your thoughts and experiences. Your feedback is like a treasure map guiding me to make things even better for those who come after you.

Your voice is important and shapes the story of this cooking adventure. Every word you share can inspire and connect with others who haven't discovered the magic in these pages yet. It's not just a review; it's a gift to others looking for a way to be healthy and happy.

So, could you take a moment to write down your thoughts? Tell me about the flavors you liked, the recipes that became your favorites, and the moments that made you smile. Your words aren't just for me; they help build a community of food lovers, each adding their unique touch to a happy and healthy life.

As you enjoy the good feelings after a tasty meal from this cookbook, know that your words can reach beyond your kitchen. They can inspire others to enjoy every meal and make every day a chance for well-being.

Thank you for more than just picking a cookbook. Thank you for becoming a part of a group of people who love good food and want to live a vibrant life.

With gratitude,

[Dr. Campbell's] ★★★★★
Publisher of the "Mediterranean Diet Cookbook for Seniors"

Chapter 9: Sweet Treats

Let's explore a delightful array of Mediterranean-inspired sweet treat recipes to satisfy your sweet tooth.

Mediterranean Orange and Almond Cake

Serving Size: 8 45 minutes

INTRODUCTION

Indulge in the citrusy delight of a Mediterranean orange and almond cake. This gluten-free treat is moist, flavorful, and perfect for any occasion.

INGREDIENTS

- Almond flour
- Oranges
- Eggs
- Honey
- Baking powder

INSTRUCTIONS

1. Boil whole oranges, then blend into a puree.
2. Mix with almond flour, eggs, honey, and baking powder.
3. Bake until golden brown.
4. Cool before slicing.

NUTRITIONAL INFORMATION:

- Calories: 220 per serving
- Protein: 8g
- Fat: 15g
- Carbohydrates: 18g

Mediterranean Yogurt Parfait

 Serving Size: 2  10 minutes

INTRODUCTION

Enjoy a light and refreshing Mediterranean yogurt parfait with layers of Greek yogurt, honey, granola, and fresh berries.

INGREDIENTS

- Greek yogurt
- Honey
- Granola
- Mixed berries

INSTRUCTIONS

1. Layer Greek yogurt in a glass.
2. Drizzle with honey and add a layer of granola.
3. Top with a mix of fresh berries.
4. Repeat layers.
5. Serve chilled.

NUTRITIONAL INFORMATION:

- Calories: 180 per serving
- Protein: 10g
- Fat: 8g
- Carbohydrates: 20g

Mediterranean Fig and Walnut Biscotti

Serving Size: 12 50 minutes

INTRODUCTION

Crunch into the perfect blend of sweetness and nuttiness with Mediterranean fig and walnut biscotti, ideal for dipping into your favorite coffee or tea.

INGREDIENTS

- All-purpose flour
- Figs, chopped
- Walnuts, chopped
- Sugar
- Eggs

INSTRUCTIONS

1. Mix flour, chopped figs, chopped walnuts, sugar, and eggs.
2. Form into a log and bake until golden.
3. Slice and bake again until crisp.
4. Allow to cool before enjoying.

NUTRITIONAL INFORMATION:

- Calories: 160 per serving
- Protein: 4g
- Fat: 7g
- Carbohydrates: 20g

Mediterranean Honey and Pistachio Baklava

Serving Size: 16 60 minutes

INTRODUCTION

Experience the decadence of Mediterranean honey and pistachio baklava, featuring layers of phyllo dough, chopped pistachios, and a sweet honey glaze.

INGREDIENTS

- Phyllo dough
- Pistachios, chopped
- Honey
- Butter
- Cinnamon

INSTRUCTIONS

1. Layer phyllo dough, melted butter, and chopped pistachios.
2. Repeat layers.
3. Bake until golden.
4. Pour honey over the warm baklava.
5. Allow to cool before cutting.

NUTRITIONAL INFORMATION:

- Calories: 200 per serving
- Protein: 5g
- Fat: 12g
- Carbohydrates: 20g

Mediterranean Lemon and Olive Oil Pound Cake

Serving Size: 10 50 minutes

INTRODUCTION

Savor the simplicity of a Mediterranean lemon and olive oil pound cake, boasting a perfect balance of citrusy brightness and rich olive oil flavor.

INGREDIENTS

- All-purpose flour
- Lemons
- Olive oil
- Sugar
- Eggs

INSTRUCTIONS

1. Mix flour, lemon zest, lemon juice, olive oil, sugar, and eggs.
2. Bake until a toothpick comes out clean.
3. Cool before slicing.

NUTRITIONAL INFORMATION:

- Calories: 240 per serving
- Protein: 5g
- Fat: 15g
- Carbohydrates: 22g

Mediterranean Orange Blossom Water Panna Cotta

Serving Size: 6 30 minutes

INTRODUCTION

Delight in the subtle floral notes of Mediterranean orange blossom water panna cotta. This creamy and aromatic dessert is a perfect way to end a Mediterranean feast.

INGREDIENTS

- Heavy cream
- Gelatin
- Sugar
- Orange blossom water

INSTRUCTIONS

1. Heat heavy cream and sugar until steaming.
2. Dissolve gelatin in the mixture.
3. Add orange blossom water.
4. Pour into molds and refrigerate until set.
5. Unmold and serve chilled.

NUTRITIONAL INFORMATION:

- Calories: 220 per serving
- Protein: 3g
- Fat: 18g
- Carbohydrates: 14g

Mediterranean Walnut and Date Truffles

Serving Size: 12 20 minutes

INTRODUCTION

Satisfy your sweet cravings with Mediterranean walnut and date truffles. These bite-sized delights are naturally sweetened and loaded with wholesome ingredients.

INGREDIENTS

- Dates, pitted
- Walnuts
- Cocoa powder
- Coconut flakes

INSTRUCTIONS

1. Blend dates and walnuts until a dough forms.
2. Shape into small balls.
3. Roll in cocoa powder or coconut flakes.
4. Chill before serving.

NUTRITIONAL INFORMATION:

- Calories: 120 per serving
- Protein: 2g
- Fat: 8g
- Carbohydrates: 12g

Mediterranean Rosewater and Pistachio Semolina Cake

Serving Size: 8 40 minutes

INTRODUCTION

Delight in the fragrant and nutty goodness of Mediterranean rosewater and pistachio semolina cake. This semolina-based dessert is a unique and delightful treat.

INGREDIENTS

- Semolina
- Pistachios, ground
- Rosewater
- Yogurt
- Sugar

INSTRUCTIONS

1. Mix semolina, ground pistachios, rosewater, yogurt, and sugar.
2. Bake until golden brown.
3. Drizzle with additional rosewater for added aroma.

NUTRITIONAL INFORMATION:

- Calories: 180 per serving
- Protein: 4g
- Fat: 7g
- Carbohydrates: 25g

Mediterranean Almond and Orange Biscotti

Serving Size: 12 50 minutes

INTRODUCTION

Pair your afternoon tea or coffee with the crunch of Mediterranean almond and orange biscotti. These twice-baked cookies are perfect for dipping.

INGREDIENTS

- Almonds, chopped
- Orange zest
- All-purpose flour
- Sugar
- Eggs

INSTRUCTIONS

1. Mix almonds, orange zest, flour, sugar, and eggs.
2. Shape into logs and bake until golden.
3. Slice and bake again until crisp.
4. Enjoy these biscotti with your favorite hot beverage.

NUTRITIONAL INFORMATION:

- Calories: 160 per serving
- Protein: 4g
- Fat: 8g
- Carbohydrates: 18g

Mediterranean Chocolate and Olive Oil Mousse

Serving Size: 6 35 minutes

INTRODUCTION

Experience the richness of Mediterranean chocolate and olive oil mousse. This velvety dessert combines the bold flavors of dark chocolate and the smoothness of olive oil.

INGREDIENTS

- Dark chocolate
- Olive oil
- Heavy cream
- Sugar

INSTRUCTIONS

1. Melt dark chocolate and olive oil together.
2. Whip heavy cream with sugar until stiff peaks form.
3. Fold the chocolate mixture into the whipped cream.
4. Chill before serving.

NUTRITIONAL INFORMATION:

- Calories: 260 per serving
- Protein: 3g
- Fat: 20g
- Carbohydrates: 18g

Mediterranean Lemon and Thyme Shortbread Cookies

Serving Size: 12 30 minutes

INTRODUCTION

Savor the delicate balance of citrusy brightness and herbal notes with Mediterranean lemon and thyme shortbread cookies. These buttery delights are perfect for an afternoon tea or as an elegant dessert.

INGREDIENTS

- All-purpose flour
- Butter
- Sugar
- Lemon zest
- Fresh thyme leaves

INSTRUCTIONS

1. Cream together butter and sugar until light and fluffy.
2. Mix in flour, lemon zest, and fresh thyme.
3. Shape into cookies and bake until golden.
4. Cool before enjoying these aromatic shortbread cookies.

NUTRITIONAL INFORMATION:

- Calories: 160 per serving
- Protein: 2g
- Fat: 10g
- Carbohydrates: 15g

Mediterranean Honey and Walnut Tart

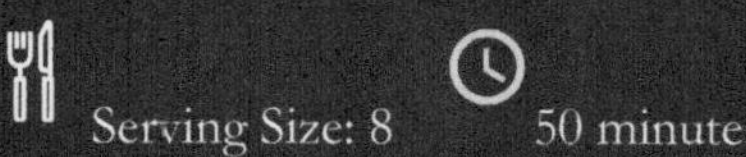

INTRODUCTION

Indulge in the rich sweetness of a Mediterranean honey and walnut tart. This classic dessert combines the earthy flavor of walnuts with the golden richness of honey.

INGREDIENTS

- Pie crust
- Walnuts, chopped
- Honey
- Brown sugar
- Butter

INSTRUCTIONS

1. Pre-bake the pie crust.
2. Mix chopped walnuts with honey, brown sugar, and melted butter.
3. Fill the pre-baked crust with the walnut mixture.
4. Bake until the filling is set.
5. Cool before slicing.

NUTRITIONAL INFORMATION:

- Calories: 280 per serving
- Protein: 5g
- Fat: 18g
- Carbohydrates: 25g

30-DAY MEDITERRANEAN DIET MEAL PLAN

CHAPTER 10: 30-DAY MEDITERRANEAN DIET MEAL PLAN

Embarking on a 30-day journey with the Mediterranean diet opens the door to a world of delicious and nutritious meals. In this chapter, we'll break down the weekly meal plan, provide comprehensive shopping lists, and offer valuable tips to ensure your success on this wholesome and flavorful adventure.

Weekly Meal Breakdown

Week 1: Embracing the Mediterranean Flavors

Day 1

- Breakfast: Greek Yogurt Parfait with Fresh Berries and Granola
- Lunch: Mediterranean Chickpea Salad
- Dinner: Grilled Lemon Herb Chicken with Quinoa and Roasted Vegetables
- Snack: Hummus with Sliced Cucumbers

Day 2

- Breakfast: Whole Grain Toast with Avocado and Poached Egg
- Lunch: Mediterranean Farro Salad with Feta and Cherry Tomatoes
- Dinner: Baked Salmon with Mediterranean Herb Marinade, Couscous, and Grilled Asparagus
- Snack: Greek Olives and Cherry Tomatoes

Day 3

- Breakfast: Spinach and Feta Omelette
- Lunch: Greek Salad with Grilled Chicken
- Dinner: Eggplant and Chickpea Stew with a Side of Whole Wheat Pita
- Snack: Mixed Nuts

Day 4

- Breakfast: Oatmeal with Fresh Berries and a Drizzle of Honey
- Lunch: Mediterranean Quinoa Bowl with Roasted Vegetables
- Dinner: Shrimp Scampi with Whole Wheat Linguine and Steamed Broccoli
- Snack: Greek Yogurt with Honey and Walnuts

Day 5

- Breakfast: Whole Grain Pancakes with Fresh Fruit
- Lunch: Tomato and Mozzarella Caprese Salad
- Dinner: Lemon Garlic Roasted Chicken Thighs with Mediterranean Couscous
- Snack: Sliced Apple with Almond Butter

Day 6

- Breakfast: Smoothie with Spinach, Banana, Greek Yogurt, and Almond Milk
- Lunch: Greek Chicken Souvlaki with Tzatziki Sauce
- Dinner: Baked Cod with Lemon and Herbs, Brown Rice, and Steamed Green Beans
- Snack: Figs and Goat Cheese

Day 7

- Breakfast: Mediterranean Frittata with Sun-Dried Tomatoes and Kalamata Olives
- Lunch: Lentil and Vegetable Stew
- Dinner: Grilled Lamb Chops with Mint Pesto, Quinoa, and Roasted Brussels Sprouts
- Snack: Roasted Red Pepper Hummus with Carrot Sticks

Week 2-4: Varied and Nutrient-Rich

The subsequent weeks will follow a similar pattern, introducing new recipes while maintaining the core principles of the Mediterranean diet. Rotate different fruits, vegetables, proteins, and grains to keep the meals exciting and diverse. Consider incorporating:

- Seafood: Explore various fish and shellfish like sardines, mussels, or grilled octopus.
- Legumes: Include more beans, lentils, and chickpeas for plant-based protein.
- Healthy Fats: Embrace the richness of olive oil, nuts, and seeds in salads, snacks, and main dishes.
- Desserts: Indulge in moderation with Mediterranean-inspired sweets like baklava, fruit salads, or yogurt-based treats.

Shopping List for Each Week

Week 1 Shopping List

Produce

- Fresh berries
- Avocado
- Spinach
- Cherry tomatoes
- Asparagus
- Eggplant
- Broccoli
- Fresh fruit (apples, figs)
- Banana
- Lemon
- Fresh herbs (thyme, rosemary, mint)

Protein

- Greek yogurt
- Chicken (breasts, thighs)
- Salmon fillets
- Shrimp
- Eggs

Grains

- Quinoa
- Whole wheat pita
- Whole grain linguine
- Farro
- Couscous
- Whole grain pancakes mix
- Brown rice

Dairy

- Feta cheese
- Mozzarella cheese
- Goat cheese

Nuts and Seeds

- Granola
- Mixed nuts
- Walnuts
- Almond butter

Legumes

- Chickpeas
- Lentils

Pantry Essentials

- Hummus
- Olives (Greek, Kalamata)
- Olive oil
- Balsamic glaze
- Honey
- Oatmeal
- Whole grain pancake mix

Week 2-4 Adjusted Shopping Lists

For subsequent weeks, adjust your shopping list based on the new recipes introduced. Explore seasonal produce and consider buying in bulk for items with a longer shelf life.

Tips for Success

Meal Prep is Key

- Spend time each week planning and preparing meals in advance.
- Batch-cook staples like quinoa, brown rice, and grilled chicken for easy assembly.

Explore Local Markets

- Visit local farmers' markets for fresh, seasonal produce.
- Experiment with unique ingredients to keep your meals exciting.

Hydration Matters

- Stay hydrated with water, herbal teas, and the occasional glass of

Mindful Eating

- Enjoy meals slowly, savoring each bite.
- Pay attention to hunger and fullness cues, promoting a healthy relationship with food.

Physical Activity

- Incorporate regular exercise, such as walking, cycling, or yoga.
- Aim for at least 150 minutes of moderate-intensity exercise per week.

Social Connection

- Share meals with friends and family, fostering a sense of community.
- Explore Mediterranean-themed potluck dinners for variety.

Mindful Indulgences

- Allow yourself occasional indulgences like a piece of dark chocolate or a small serving of dessert.
- Balance is key; savor the treats without guilt.

Adapt to Preferences

- Tailor the meal plan to your preferences and dietary needs.
- Experiment with vegetarian or vegan options if desired

Listen to Your Body

- Pay attention to how different foods make you feel.
- Adjust portion sizes based on hunger and satisfaction.

Celebrate Progress

- Celebrate milestones and small victories during your 30-day journey.
- Reflect on the positive changes in energy, mood, and overall well-being.

By embracing the Mediterranean diet with a thoughtful approach, you're not just adopting a meal plan; you're adopting a lifestyle. Enjoy the process, celebrate the flavors, and reap the benefits of this wholesome and sustainable way of eating. Bon appétit!

Conclusion

Congratulations on completing your journey through "Mediterranean Delights: The Complete Simple and Easy Delicious Recipes for Seniors 2024"! This culinary adventure has not only filled your kitchen with the enticing aromas of Mediterranean cuisine but has also nourished your body and soul with wholesome, flavorful meals. the Mediterranean diet isn't just a collection of recipes; it's a lifestyle that celebrates the joy of nourishing both the body and the soul. As you continue your culinary exploration, may the flavors of the Mediterranean continue to bring vibrancy and vitality to your everyday life. Thank you for choosing "Mediterranean Delights," and we look forward to accompanying you on future adventures in the world of wholesome and delicious cuisine. Bon appétit!

Thank You